FRUIT OF THE SPIRIT

MW00331994

KINDNESS

Fruit of the Spirit Study Guide Series

Love

Joy

Peace

Patience

Kindness

Goodness

Faithfulness

Gentleness

Self-Control

CALVIN MILLER

 FRUIT OF THE SPIRIT

KINDNESS

Published in Nashville, Tennessee, by Thomas Nelson. Thomas Nelson is a trademark of Thomas Nelson, Inc.

Typesetting by Gregory C. Benoit Publishing, Old Mystic, CT

Thomas Nelson, Inc., titles may be purchased in bulk for educational, business, fund-raising, or sales promotional use. For information, please e-mail SpecialMarkets@ThomasNelson.com.

ISBN: 978-1-4185-2837-9

Printed in the United States of America
09 10 11 12 QW 7 6 5 4 3 2

TABLE OF CONTENTS

But the fruit of the Spirit is love, joy, peace, patience, kind-ness, goodness, faithfulness, gentleness and self-control. Against such things there is no law.
—Galatians 5:22–23

INTRODUCTION

Like the other fruits of the Spirit, kindness is a characteristic of God. Because God is kind, he saved Noah and his family from the flood. Because God is kind, he confused the languages of the people at Babel rather than destroying them for trying to build a tower to reach the heavens. Because God is kind, you and I breathe and live. There is no other explanation.

When we see God's Spirit overwhelm a person, that person naturally will be kind. Paul told the Philippians not to think too highly of themselves. We are to consider others before we consider ourselves. That is the essence of kindness we are called to embody.

Why aren't people kind? There are plenty of reasons, but the basic reason is that they don't have a relationship with God. Servers in restaurants often report that they would rather work any day other than Sunday. Why? Because the church people are the most demanding and rudest customers they have. In addition, they're bad tippers! What a sad commentary on the depth to which God penetrates the souls of those who claim to be his followers. Those people have yet to let God enter their lives. They aren't followers of God; they are fans of God. Which are you?

You can't seek to become kind; you seek God and kindness is the result. Kindness happens when we put aside our selfish ways and allow God to call the shots. Kindness draws people to faith relationships with God; meanness pushes them away. Just hanging around the church doesn't make someone kind. Going to a small group, singing in the choir, being a teacher, or rocking babies won't do it either. Kindness isn't a result of what we do; it is a result of whose we are.

When we belong to us, we can't be kind. When we belong to God, we can't help but be kind. As we go through this study together, we will reevaluate the ownership of our lives and determine if God really owns us. The Bible says we were bought with a price and that we no longer belong to ourselves. Are you letting your new owner run the show? Let's see what God has to say!

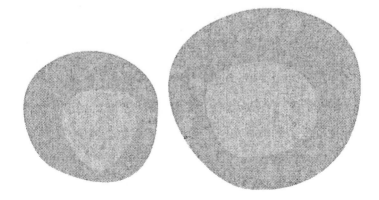

HOW TO USE THIS GUIDE

Galatians 5:22–23 is not a plan to achieve better faith. Rather, it is a description of God's personal gifts to all of us. If we follow God and seek his blessing, then the fruits of the Spirit are a natural overflow in our relationship with God. We are to grow in character so that one day we will reflect the image of our Lord.

This series of nine six-week studies will clearly focus your spiritual life to become more like Christ. Each study guide is divided into six weeks, and each of the six-week courses covers one of the fruits of the Spirit. Participants simply read each daily study and answer the questions at the end of each devotional. This prepares everyone for the group discussion at the end of the week.

Each week features a similar pattern that explores one aspect of that study's fruit of the Spirit. The first lesson establishes the aspect of the fruit to be explored throughout the week. The second lesson looks at the week's theme as it relates to God's purpose in the life of the believer. The third lesson looks at the week's theme as it relates to the believer's relationship with Christ. The fourth lesson explores how the fruit is relevant in service to others. And in the fifth lesson, the theme is related to personal worship. A sixth lesson is included as a bonus study, and focuses on either a biblical character who modeled this particular fruit, or a key parable that brings the theme into focus.

Each weeklong study should conclude in a group review. The weekly group discussion serves as a place to understand the practical side of the theme and receive encouragement and feedback on the journey to become more Christlike. For the study to have the character-transforming effect God desires, it is important for the participant to spend ten to twenty minutes a day reading the Scripture passage and the devotional, and to think through the two questions for the day. If each participant reads all of the questions beforehand, it greatly enhances the group dynamic. Each participant should choose three or four questions to discuss during the group session.

These simple guidelines will help make group time productive. Take a total of about forty-five minutes to answer and discuss the questions. Each person need not answer every question, but be sure all members participate. You can stimulate participation by having everyone respond to an icebreaker question. Have each group member answer the first of the six questions listed at the end of the week, and leave the remaining questions open-ended. Or, make up your own icebreaker question, such as: What color best represents the day you are having? What is your favorite movie? Or, how old were you when you had your first kiss?

No one should respond to all of the questions. Keep in mind that if you are always talking, the others are not. It is essential that everyone contribute. If you notice that someone is not participating, ask that group member which question is the most relevant. Be sensitive if something is keeping that member from contributing. Don't ask someone to read or pray aloud unless you know that the member is comfortable with such a task.

Always start and end your time with prayer. Sometimes it helps to have each person say what he or she plans to do with the lesson that week. Remember to reserve ten minutes for group prayer. You might want to keep a list of requests and answers to prayer at the back of this book.

Week 1: Kindness as a Worldview

Memory Passage for the Week: Ephesians 4:32

Day 1: Kindness as a Worldview

Kindness is the great virtue of the Christian life. 2 Samuel 9:1–10.

Day 2: The Purpose of God in My Life

It cannot be said too often: both kindness and gentleness are the call of God for every life. Deuteronomy 10:17–19.

Day 3: My Relationship with Christ

Kindness heightens our own relationship with Christ. It could be that kind people cry more easily than the unconcerned. Kindness is the virtue of empathy. Matthew 23:37–39.

Day 4: My Service to Others

Cultural unkindness is cultural apathy. Cultural apathy is "every person for himself." This is the last state of cultural degradation. Amos 5:11–13.

Day 5: My Personal Worship

Worship is only valuable when it comes from real, warm human beings. Matthew 5:24.

Day 6: A Character Study on Rahab

Joshua 2:1–21; 6:22–25

Day 7: Group Discussion

Day 1: Kindness as a Worldview
Read 2 Samuel 9:1–10

After years of purging the house of Saul, David finally asked, "Is there anyone still left of the house of Saul to whom I can show kindness?" (2 Samuel 9:1). Yes, there is always somebody to whom we can show kindness. In this case it was Mephibosheth, Jonathan's son. Jonathan was David's best friend, and just the knowledge that his son was in need touched the king's heart. Mephibosheth became crippled as a little boy when his nurse dropped him (2 Samuel 4:4). David's desire that his own family be the new monarchy made Saul's house unwelcome in Israel, including Mephibosheth. Mephibosheth lived in the land of Lo-De-Bar. The word *Lo-De-Bar* means "No Pasture," indicating that Jonathan's son was living in great need.

But David welcomed Mephibosheth to the palace. The outcast met grace; the disabled man without human support lived and dined at the king's table.

Kindness is the great virtue of the Christian life. Kindness is usually so automatic, so basic to our nature, that those who are kindest among us do not suspect themselves as kind. Watch people whom regularly open doors for the elderly—they smile once the act is completed and hurry about their business, never seeing the glory in their simple deed. In essence, Christlike kindness never stops to celebrate itself.

Bellhops, flight attendants, and waiters all provide the sort of kindness that is paid for and professional. But the people we like best are those whose kindness is not purchased, but who behave this way just for the joy of it. That Christlike kindness changes the world. It melts the hearts of gladiators. It lifts spiritual orphans toward the Fatherhood of God. It smiles in a sea of frowns. It says, "What can I do to help you?" and actually hopes to be given an assignment. Kindness wears sandals—it has since the first century.

Questions for Personal Reflection

1. Describe a time you were the recipient of Christlike kindness.

When I was hospitalized in Ar - 50 cards & food + visits + prayers

2. What are some ways in which you can show Christlike kindness to someone today?

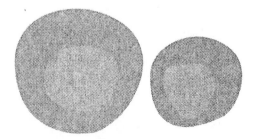

Day 2: The Purpose of God in My Life

Read Deuteronomy 10:17–19

As we read the Pentateuch, we must be careful to see more than just the "legal side" of God. In Deuteronomy, the Lord quit saying, "Thou shalt not," and began saying, "Go to it." Instead of telling Israel how to keep from sinning, God dealt with a more subtle kind of sin—the sin of omission. It is a sin to fail to defend the cause of the orphan. So is the failure to protect widows. So is the failure to help the foreigner who suffers from severe loneliness in a strange culture.

I was once victimized by thieves in Spain. I remember the ordeal of having to go to a civil court and listen to the proceedings in Spanish, none of which I understood. It hurt to be a stranger in a strange land. I had the odd feeling of being central to a court scene without the slightest ability to understand or defend myself.

Here in this Deuteronomy passage is found a kind of Golden Rule litany that occurs often in the Pentateuch: "For you yourselves were ..." (Deuteronomy 10:19). How frequently are we intolerant of those people who are now as we once were? Who is harder on alcoholics than former drunks? Who is more severe on divorce than those who once came close to divorce themselves? If saints have any single, glaring unkindness, it is their failure to forgive others in ways that they themselves have been forgiven.

If it seems nothing can motivate you to be kind, remember the moral of Deuteronomy: "You yourselves [once] were _____." Now fill in the blank with an honest confession and treat others as you wish you were treated when you endured the same thing.

Questions for Personal Reflection

1. Are there sins of omission in your own life? What are they?

2. Are there specific sins toward which your attitude is different than God's attitude? If so, what are some things you can do to let God transform your attitude?

Day 3: My Relationship with Christ
Read Matthew 23:37–39

Jesus was weeping! Tears are a sign of kindness. In fact, tears often precede kindness. We see some pitiable situation, and we cry. Whether our tears fall on the outside or on the inside, they will fall somewhere.

Jesus wept over the citadel, but the citadel never knew. Those who rejoice at our kindness rarely suspect our tears.

It has long haunted me that in the years before I was saved, my incognito Lord wept over my condition until at last I came to him. Those in Jerusalem who never suspected Christ's weeping were little different from us. The truth is that God weeps daily for all who are lost. He still cries over all who are self-serving, who never suspect that there are any larger reasons for their lives.

When such a need to be kind exists in the human heart, the person possessed of such kindness becomes a stalker of grace. He or she moves into the world serving a wonderful—and sometimes desperate—agenda: *What can I do to serve Christ? What can I do to make the world a better place? What can I do to all of those I see in need?* We don't actually do it for the sake of others. We do it as unto Christ.

The result? Well, we become more like Jesus. I've often gloried over those Jesus met casually along the way—the blind, for instance. In random acts of kindness Jesus gave to the needy, for no other reason than they were the children of God. They went home healed.

Kindness—instant and unstoppable—heals the world.

Questions for Personal Reflection

1. In what ways have you been healed?

2. How can God use you to bring healing to someone in need of it?

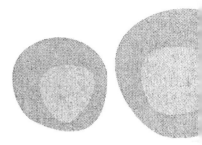

Day 4: My Service to Others
Read Amos 5:11–13

Amos showed us what kindness is by telling a story of unkindness. The unkind trampled the poor, refused to help, and all the while built stone mansions, elaborately landscaped with lush vineyards. The problem with wealth is that it can dull people's minds into believing everyone's lifestyle is just like theirs. Nothing keeps us from noticing the hurt of the hurting like the magnification of our own comfort.

It is believed that Marie Antoinette, when told that her starving people had no bread, replied, "Well, let them eat cake!" Such a statement presupposed life in a French palace where, if the larders were low on one food, one might merely select another menu item. Marie Antoinette was like the wealthy people of Israel. Blinded by their own wealthy, indulgent lifestyles, they could not see that the vast majority of their countrymen had neither bread—nor cake.

In 1999 when NATO acted to help the Kosovars, one can easily imagine the ones who objected most violently to U.S. involvement in this international struggle objecting from plush armchairs while channel-surfing their way between newscasts in air-conditioned homes. Meanwhile, hundreds of thousands lived in floorless tents in a sea of icy mud. American Christians are not wholly innocent of the blasé mystique. Christians who live in their own well-furnished homes and travel to worship in nice cars may not truly feel Kosovo's pain.

Kindness is our willingness to care about others who may not have our standard of living and may even live one comfortable ocean-moat away from our luxurious lifestyles.

Questions for Personal Reflection

1. Describe a time when you've noticed someone's relative wealth make them insensitive to others. Have you ever been on the giving or receiving end of this kind of insensitivity? Explain.

2. What are three places you can go to find the needy in your community? Once there, what are some things you can do to help meet their needs?

Homeless shelter - serve meals, talk to them
Food pantry - Fill boxes or sacks for needy famil

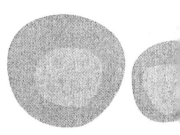

Day 5: My Personal Worship
Read Matthew 5:24

Jesus counseled all quarrelsome worshipers to be reconciled before they came to worship: "Leave your gift there in front of the altar ... and be reconciled to your brother" (Matthew 5:24). The world sometimes is guilty of coming to worship and trying to present God with a heart of loving admiration while trying to inflate its own reputation.

The church historically has been guilty of what James calls "fights and quarrels among you" (James 4:1). In your church, when visitors come to worship, do they find members who extend kindness to each other and the visitors in their midst? Or would visitors be far more likely to find the church embroiled in a quarrel that, for the most part, prevents them from seeing the stranger in their midst?

Grudges and harsh viewpoints don't just keep us from seeing visitors; they keep us from seeing God. John put it this way in 1 John 4:20: "If anyone says, 'I love God,' yet hates his brother, he is a liar. For anyone who does not love his brother, whom he has seen, cannot love God, whom he has not seen." From what John says, it is safe to assume that many angry worshipers may come to church and never see God at all.

Kind people, on the other hand, enter worship with no human biases against others. Loving all others is the first step toward giving uncontaminated love to God. From the high, thin air of exalted worship, those who love can see directly into heaven. Their own kind hearts enable them to see the great God of Isaiah 6: high and exalted (v. 1). For them, he is always high and lifted up. They worship and live in such joy that they never see any contradiction between their own kind nature and the level of adoration they give God. Indeed there is no contradiction.

Questions for Personal Reflection

1. How do harsh thoughts and grudges affect your ability to work? How do they affect your ability to worship?

2. Can you think of any arguments or grudges you should resolve? What are they? How can you begin reconciling relationships?

Day 6: Rahab—The Scarlet Cord of Promise

Read Joshua 2:1–21; 6:22–25

Kindness alone spared the prostitute Rahab. But her kindness also gave her an enduring niche in Hebrew history. Kindness has the power to fix us into permanence if we give it a place of deep influence in our lives. Rahab noticed God's greatness in Israel's journey from Egypt to the borders of Canaan. Rahab knew that number of people could never escape Pharaoh's clutches and live in the less-than-accommodating rigors of Sinai unless their God was "the" God. "I know that the LORD has given this land to you," said Rahab, "and that a great fear of you has fallen on us, so that all who live in this country are melting in fear because of you. We have heard how the LORD dried up the water of the Red Sea for you when you came out of Egypt, and what you did to Sihon and Og, the two kings of the Amorites east of the Jordan, whom you completely destroyed" (Joshua 2:9–10). So she may not have been merely kind to the spies. She was probably just plain smart, and provided for her own security by kindly helping them escape from Jericho's local authorities.

Still, kindness begets kindness. Rahab befriended the spies, who reciprocated by promising to spare Rahab when they conquered Jericho. Rahab simply asked, "Now then, please swear to me by the LORD that you will show kindness to my family, because I have shown kindness to you. Give me a sure sign that you will spare the lives of my father and mother,

[handwritten note: Vital info. To the 2 spies sent by Joshua to Jericho.]

my brothers and sisters, and all who belong to them, and that you will save us from death" (vv. 12–13).

The sign was set: she was to tie a scarlet cord in her window (v. 18) and when the men returned for the siege of Jericho, they saw the scarlet cord and spared Rahab's entire family in the day of slaughter. This scarlet cord was the sign of kindness. Rahab both gave and received kindness.

Jericho was conquered!

"Joshua said to the two men who had spied out the land, 'Go into the prostitute's house and bring her out and all who belong to her, in accordance with your oath to her.' So the young men who had done the spying went in and brought out Rahab, her father and mother and brothers and all who belonged to her ... and she lives among the Israelites to this day" (Joshua 6:22–25).

In time, this one simple kindness wound its scarlet cord into the very lineage of Christ (Matthew 1:5).

Kindness pays dividends here in this life, yet it is no mere political maneuver.

It smiles to reassure the frightened.

It holds out bread to the starving.

It is an oasis in the desert of "everybody's got to make a living."

It is a banquet in the famine of "God helps those who help themselves."

Questions for Personal Reflection

1. Have you ever done something nice for someone, hoping they would

reciprocate? What was it? How did you feel afterward?

2. What is the ultimate expression of kindness? How can you live in response to
that?

Doing for someone not expecting anything in return

Day 7: Group Discussion

The following questions should take about forty-five minutes to answer
and discuss. Each member should answer the first question, leaving the
remaining questions open-ended. Everyone need not answer, but be sure
all members participate.

1.   *When you consider acts of kindness, what examples come to mind?*

Offering a friend a ride
Taking food to someone who has lost a loved
one -
Letting someone ahead of you in a checkout line
who seems to be running late.
Welcoming new neighbor w/ bread loaf or cookies.

2.   *Think about an occasion when you hesitated to help someone. What made it dif-*
     ficult for you to act on impulse? What helped you overcome this difficulty?

3. *Why is it hard for some people to receive kindness? Is it hard for you? Why?*

They are not Christians + don't know the teachings of Jesus.
Kindness comes from love of God

"Let Others See Jesus In Me"

4. *How has Jesus' death for our sins affected your life? How does it affect your everyday life?*

All of my sins are forgiven because of His kindness to me. I try to be Christ-like to others so they may see Christ in me.

5. Sometimes showing kindness is harder than it sounds. What are some situations where it's harder to show kindness? How can you allow God to be kind through you? *prayer   wwjd*

6. Because kindness is a fruit of the Spirit, its presence in you can indicate your spiritual health. Based on personal kindness, how healthy are you spiritually? Are you satisfied with that level? If not, how can you improve? *I think there is always room for improvement.*

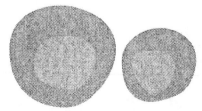

Week 2: Kindness in the Time of Need

Memory Passage for the Week: Jeremiah 9:23–24

Day 1: Kindness in the Time of Need

Showing kindness to others in their time of need automatically reflects the kindness of Jesus. Joshua 2:8–14.

Day 2: The Purpose of God in My Life

In spite of his tremendous suffering, Job saw God as the Lord of kindness. Job 10:12.

Day 3: My Relationship with Christ

The apostle Paul taught that God does not approve of those who have been forgiven of great sin and yet are stingy in their ability to return kindness to those they judge. Romans 2:3–4.

Day 4: My Service to Others

Even small gifts—when given from the heart—exhibit a kindness for which the giver will be rewarded. Matthew 10:40–42.

Day 5: My Personal Worship

Isaiah, who often celebrated the grand themes of exile, stopped to celebrate the kindness of the great Jehovah. Isaiah 63:7.

Day 6: A Character Study on Esther

Esther 4:15–17; 5:4–7; 7:3–4; 8:5

Day 7: Group Discussion

Day 1: Kindness in the Time of Need
Read Joshua 2:8–14

Our last character study examined the surprising kindness of the prostitute, Rahab. "Kindness in a time of need" may have been Rahab's motto. Most people probably did not expect someone like Rahab to show such abundant kindness. She was a prostitute, a Gentile, and ... yes, a liar. Yet hidden beneath her faults—as her Israelite guests found out—was a woman capable of kindness—and not just any kindness, but kindness in a time of great need.

We all know what it is like to be in need of kindness. One night, after the train I was riding through India derailed, I found myself on a cold stretch of unfamiliar highway seventy miles south of Delhi. It was near midnight, and I did not know a single word of Hindi. After several vain attempts to flag down a cattle truck, a rather well dressed, clearly upper-caste Hindu man approached and offered me a ride back to my hotel in the city. I was overjoyed by his kindness. On the way, I discovered he was a devout Hindu and was currently celebrating the feasts of the nine goddesses. He was a reincarnationist, and strongly held to the caste system, an abomination I despised. Like Rahab, there were many things wrong, but he showed me kindness in a time of need.

Even a pagan man in such circumstances caused me to think of Jesus. We cannot underestimate the power of showing kindness to someone in need. Jesus, in his time on earth, was drawn to and showed great compassion toward people who were in great need, whether physical, emotional, or spiritual. When we show compassion and kindness to those around us, Jesus' heart inevitably shines through us.

Questions for Personal Reflection

1. Describe a time when you have been shown kindness in a time of great need.

2. Think of a time when you were shown kindness by someone you would have never expected. How did that kindness you were shown impact you?

Day 2: The Purpose of God in My Life

Read Job 10:12

The kindness of God endears us to him and, according to Job, he makes his kindness obvious through his providence. God does provide. Our daily bread would not be buttered without his providence. Job, whom, it seemed, got only tough times from God, spoke of the amazing and wonderful ways God creates and takes care of us:

> *Your hands shaped me and made me.*
> *Will you now turn and destroy me?*
> *Remember that you molded me like clay.*
> *Will you now turn me to dust again?*
> *Did you not pour me out like milk*
> *and curdle me like cheese,*
> *clothe me with skin and flesh*
> *and knit me together with bones and sinews?*
> —Job 10:8–11

Lost in the wonders of God's creativity, Job had to reckon with all the difficult things that happened to him. There was a kind of harmony suggested here. Would a God who carefully shaped and created us turn and destroy us? Job didn't think so. God is consistently love, so we must not be quick to indict him for all our misfortunes. Let us rather see if we can read into our pain a bit of his larger purpose. When the pain is bad, we may struggle harder to see his deeper purpose, but it must be our goal. In all things, we must strive to see the kindness of God and ponder his purposes in our lives.

Questions for Personal Reflection

1. Recall a time when your suffering caused you to question God's purpose and plan for you. How did that situation affect your relationship with God?

2. What words of encouragement might help someone struggling to find meaning in his or her suffering?

Day 3: My Relationship with Christ

Read Romans 2:3–4

God is kind because it is his nature as a loving God. But this kindness has a fringe benefit. It draws us into relationship with Christ.

To reject God's kindness is to hurt our relationship with Christ. For God loved the world so much that his kindness was spent to the very last drop of Christ's blood. The major question for sinful humanity must be, "Was this selfish planet worth it?"

Theologians sometimes refer to this as the burden of God. God created humanity to glorify him, but humanity didn't. In fact, this rebellion forced him to answer sin with his Son's life.

The mother of the singer in my parable entitled *A Symphony in Sand* stands at the foot of the gallows that claims the life of her son and asks:

> *"O Son, was the planet worth all this?"*
> *She gestured to His dying form,*
> *"Should love bleed out its last for worlds*
> *Too self-concerned to pity all its whispers*
> *When it has lost the volume of its voice?*
> *You loved but have no lovers.*
> *Where are all those for whom this price is paid?"*[1]

The kindness of God is there to lead the world to repentance. Each of us desperately needs that kindness. Those who see the kindness of Calvary and walk past it unchanged pay such a heavy price.

Questions for Personal Reflection

1. Describe your first encounter with Calvary's kindness. How were you changed?

2. In what ways are you daily affected by God's kindness?

He walks with me, beside me, protects me, guides me, gives me opportunities to be like Him to others—

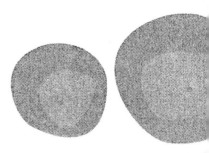

Day 4: My Service to Others
Read Matthew 10:40–42

Can our service to others be summed up in something so simple as a cup of water? Yes, it can. It is not the water but the giver's kindness that causes us to notice the universal thirst of the dying world around us.

Jesus pointed this out to the Samaritan woman at the well. The world needs living water. The only source of such refreshment is Jesus.

In "The Rhyme of the Ancient Mariner," Samuel Taylor Coleridge lamented the fate of his fabled Mariner, trapped on a windless sea. He was dying. Not a hint of breeze came to give the slightest billow to his sails. The vast sea wore the moss and slime of an English moor. The ocean was a breathless swamp. The water in which the ship sat couldn't even offer them a fresh drink. The Mariner lamented:

> *Day after day, day after day, we stuck nor breath nor motion,*
> *As idle as a painted ship upon a painted ocean.*
> *Water, water everywhere and all the boards did shrink.*
> *Water, water everywhere, nor any drop to drink.*

Did Coleridge merely lament a mythical, fictional ship, or was he talking about a world where the days were dry and any refreshment was hopeless?

So Jesus—who called himself the Living Water—became this very offering, his salvation freely, kindly given. This is our service to God, our service to others. We are the water bearers in the vast cultural deserts we are charged to save.

Questions for Personal Reflection

1. What are some situations in which you might have the opportunity to be a water bearer?

2. How might a cup of water affect someone else's spiritual life?

Day 5: My Personal Worship

Read Isaiah 63:7

Isaiah saw that we cannot enter into a time of worship unless the enduring presence of God's kindness beckons us in. The ultimate kindness of
Calvary leads us to the highest altar of personal worship. When we take
time to quietly adore Jesus on our own—one on one—sooner or later we
come to the cross. It is nearly impossible to remain spiritually blind like
the two disciples on the road to Emmaus, who couldn't see Jesus right in
front of them. When we get a revelation of his nail-scarred hands, the
kindness that leads us to salvation causes our quiet personal worship to
soar.

I wrote in my journal during this kind of personal, quiet-time rapture
in 1986:

> *Hands. Broken, leathery, big and tough,*
> *And weathered, hammer-gripping, sweating fists,*
> *Quite used to driving nails into the rough*
> *And bronze, blue-bruised where once the iron missed.*
> *A hand's a thing of beauty, in the eye*
> *Of those who, vision-trained, can pierce the skin*
> *To see the steel of sturdy bones laid white,*
> *And fragile tendons, filament and thin.*

The riddle of the nails I understand—
How leathered calluses breed tougher skin,
Hiding tiny porcelain machines within
The flesh of your strong, injured, suff'ring hands.

Your hammer-wielding fists at last grew frail
And beckoned to each palm a killing nail.[2]

It is altogether fitting that our quiet time should end here, at the Cross. Now we know God's kindness goes farther than we'd ever dreamed. It sees our lostness, considers our unworthiness, and dies for us anyway. Hallelujah!

Questions for Personal Reflection

1. Pause for a moment and reflect on God's incredible love for you. What comes to mind?

2. How can you express your love to God?

Day 6: Esther—The Soft Underbelly of Courage Is Kindness

Read Esther 4:15–17, 5:4–7, 7:3–4, 8:5

Esther was adopted, raised by her cousin Mordecai, brought into Xerxes' harem, and made queen as the result of winning a sort of beauty contest. In a radical attempt at genocide, Haman, Persia's sneakiest villain, hatched a plot to completely exterminate the Jews. Esther learned of the plot and acted in a bold way to save her people. This wonderful story is a tale of courage, and it teaches that the underbelly of courage is kindness. It is said that courage is fear that has said its prayers (which is exactly what Esther asked of her people before her daring approach to Xerxes in Esther 5:1–2). Esther approached Xerxes four times, each time initiating her requests with the tenuous word "if."

1. *"If it pleases the king ... let the king, together with Haman, come today to a banquet I have prepared for him"* (Esther 5:4 emphasis mine). Such a tenuous beginning was extremely kind in lieu of all the things she planned to achieve.
2. *"If the king regards me with favor"* (Esther 5:8 emphasis mine). Esther said this again cautiously, kindly making an appeal to Xerxes to attend her banquet.
3. *"If I have found favor with you, O king"* (Esther 7:3 emphasis mine). The queen pleaded kindly as she was about to make her great move of courage in denouncing Haman.

4. "If *it pleases the king*" (Esther 8:5 emphasis mine). Each of these beginnings shows that Esther used courage mixed with kindness. Blatant courage can offend people and sometimes doesn't get the job done—but kind courage achieves what brashness cannot.

Esther is remembered for having said, "I will go to the king, even though it is against the law. And if I perish, I perish" (Esther 4:16). But what she really meant was, "I will go to the king and kindly but courageously make my case. Then if I perish, so be it."

Kindness and courage add up to charisma. Kindness is the simple act of putting others before ourselves. Such kindness is what the Hebrews called *chesed,* a synonym for *grace.* The New Testament word for "grace" is *charis,* which means "gift." Giving is what you do when you put others ahead of yourself. Kindness includes all of these things.

Questions for Personal Reflection

1. Describe a time you exercised courage without kindness. How did your

actions affect those around you? How might kindness have changed things?

When Wally tried to shoot himself

2. What are some situations in which you need courage? How does your

personal relationship with God equip you to face these situations?

Day 7: Group Discussion

The following questions should take about forty-five minutes to answer and discuss. Each member should answer the first question, leaving the remaining questions open-ended. Everyone need not answer, but be sure all members participate.

1. *Who in your life exemplifies kindness? Explain.*

   Grandmother - early in life.

2. *When were you in a situation where you expected kindness from someone but were disappointed? How did that affect you? What lesson can you apply to your own life?*

3. If you show someone kindness, what might he or she assume about your relation-
    ship with God? ~~That you have allowed God's~~
    ~~want to plant.~~ ~~That~~

4. What are some unlikely situations in which you experienced godly kindness?

5. How would you respond to someone who suggests that God is too kind to hold us accountable for sin? God is holy. pure, maker of all things, without sin - Sin comes between you + God. God can not tolerate sin so after Adam sinned in the garden, God loved us so much that He had to find a way that we could come to Him even though we are sinners so He sent us His Son Jesus as a sacrifice for our sins. He took all of our sins on himself

6. What can you do to think of selfless kindness over your own needs and desires? Ask God to guide you in that direction. Inquire about needs of those in your church family, neighborhood or community,

Week 3: Kindness—Anger Washed by Grace

Memory Passage for the Week: Ephesians 4:26

Day 1: Kindness—Anger Washed by Grace

Once we are washed clean by God's grace, we are naturally more kind.
2 Kings 5:1, 9–15.

Day 2: The Purpose of God in My Life

When we allow God to calm our tempers, we can once again be capable
of great kindness. Proverbs 16:32.

Day 3: My Relationship with Christ

Peter chopped off a servant's ear in a foolish attempt to defend Christ.
Jesus told him to put up his sword. Such unkindness was pitiful in light of
all Christ came to achieve. John 18:10–11.

Day 4: My Service to Others

Sometimes the most diseased of souls may become kind when their
grudges are washed by the grace of God. 2 Kings 7:3–11.

Day 5: My Personal Worship

When you clean away hate, love will fit perfectly in the space you've
cleared. Psalms 137:8–9; 138:1.

Day 6: A Character Study on Aquila and Priscilla

Acts 18:1–4, 18–22, 24–26; Romans 16:3–5; 1 Corinthians 16:19

Day 7: Group Discussion

Day 1: Kindness—Anger Washed by Grace
Read 2 Kings 5:1, 9–15

Kindness does not always wear a benevolent smile. As Shakespeare said in quite another context, sometimes God "must be cruel if only to be kind." God's requirements sometimes seem severe, and we grow angry and refuse to obey Him.

Naaman received the prescription for his healing, and at first, rejected it. The prophet's command for him to dip into the Jordan was not to his liking. He wanted to be free of leprosy, but hoped his healing would come in a dramatic form that both cured him and allowed him to keep his dignity.

One would think a leper would have so little dignity that any healing would be more than adequate. Still, this leper became angry. Eroded and disfigured, Naaman raged at God's unusual requirement. This angry leper failed to see that a cure is an act of grace. Yet Naaman's ego survived to the last, still somewhat in the way of God's cleansing. The metaphor fits all of us. Most people—drowning in sin and in need of God—make demands rather than yield to his instructions. If God says simply, "Look and live," we would rather live some other way than having to look to do it.

Because lepers had very few options, Naaman finally obeyed. Then his stormy anger was calmed by obedience. He was washed by grace. Once he was clean, he became kind. He begged the prophet, "Please, accept now a gift from your servant" (2 Kings 5:15). His hostility was gone; he actually *was* kind.

There is a domesticating force in the heart of grace. Once we obey God, our wild ego struggles can rest. We find our anger has an understanding heart. We can—like Naaman—minister to those we once considered enemies.

Questions for Personal Reflection

1. What are some reasons you have been angry at God?

2. How did God's kindness penetrate your life and your heart?

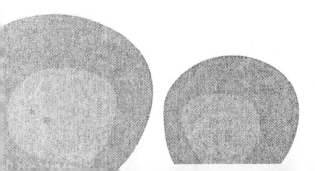

Day 2: The Purpose of God in My Life
Read Proverbs 16:32

This proverb seems to preach patience more than kindness, but consider its instruction in a deeper way. Examine the proverbs right before and right after Proverbs 16:32:

> **Proverbs 16:31:** "Gray hair is a crown of splendor; it is attained by a righteous life."
>
> **Proverbs 16:33:** "The lot is cast into the lap, but its every decision is from the LORD."

All three of these proverbs, taken at once, seem to speak of a lifestyle controlled by God. Kindness is the hallmark of God's control of our lives.

People who submit to God's control exhibit this grace. What is the evidence of kindness? Kind people are interruptible. They can stop what they are doing and care for others. Jesus' biography appears sometimes a haphazard hodgepodge of good deeds. His compassion allowed him to be interrupted by anyone else's need. His great heart of kindness could not pass up a call for help. So he established the kingdom, but never by being unkind to the needy who thronged his ministry.

Kindness endears us to a cold world that runs desperately short on selflessness. Peter wrote, "Dear friends, I urge you, as aliens and strangers in the world, to abstain from sinful desires, which war against your soul. Live such good lives among the pagans that, though they accuse you of doing wrong, they may see your good deeds and glorify God on the day he visits us" (1 Peter 2:11–12).

The world looks for kindness. They will hear and trust those who practice kindness. And once they warm up to us, God opens a door for us to minister to them, bringing God close to those who need him.

Questions for Personal Reflection

1. If kindness is the hallmark of God's control of your life, is his influence obvious in your behavior?

2. Consider your workplace or neighborhood. Who could use a touch of kindness? How can you deliver that kindness?

Day 3: My Relationship with Christ

Read John 18:10–11

In his own mind, the motive behind Peter's ear-chopping defense of Jesus probably made sense. But he did it out of anger, and Jesus rebuked Peter and reminded him of the true nature of power and submission.

When it came to combat, Peter made a good . . . fisherman! One might wonder why Peter suddenly launched into a swashbuckling foray, when not once in three years had Jesus trained his disciples in the art of war. Jesus had, after all, called Peter to fish for men (Matthew 4:19), not to hack up kingdom opponents. If it weren't such a sad story, Peter's terrible fencing skills would almost be funny.

This ear-hacking probably didn't strike Malchus as an act of kindness (it's generally hard to like anyone who hacks off your ear). The worse part of this sin is that Jesus did not command Peter to do a little swashbuckling to prove his commitment. That was Peter's own idea.

In another account, Jesus healed Malchus's severed ear, but the incident could not have made Peter and Malchus bosom buddies. It is hard to evangelize the earless when we made them so. Kindness leaves the ears intact.

Years later, perhaps this reminded Peter that when one acts without Christ's command, he usually succeeds only in foolish and trivial conduct. What we do is not only unkind, it is always rash if we act without the orders of our Master.

Questions for Personal Reflection

1. What are some of the situations in which you have acted without regard for Jesus' instructions? *Kelly late night entry*

2. How does God communicate his instructions to you? How important is it for you to spend time getting God's instructions? *very - He wants His best for us. The still small voice (conscience)*

Day 4: My Service to Others
Read 2 Kings 7:3–11

The Italians have a fable about a toy maker who fashioned a very disobe-dient marionette. From the moment Pinocchio gained independence, it was a major problem for Gepetto, his creator.

Pinocchio wanted to live without strings, but he used his freedom as a cloak of maliciousness and refused to do anything his maker asked. This disobedience constantly insulted his creator's love for him. Finally, the marionette was involved with the shadiest of characters. When he lied, his nose grew like a kind of visible polygraph. Everyone saw his sin. He wasn't what his maker created him to be. So the tale parallels God's cre-ation of us. Only grace prevents our becoming what God never intended us to be.

Consider the story of Naaman in 2 Kings, chapter 5. No doubt these lepers wanted a life without leprosy—they wanted to be free of sickness and impending death. In their debilitating condition, they cared about a world that called them unclean outcasts. Yet grace makes its require-ments even on lepers.

Naaman's stiff heart ultimately yielded. He obeyed God. Down, down, down into Jordan he went. Seven times. Each time he came up, his leprous flesh was still stained brown by the muddy river—a therapy he despised—he longed for the clean, clear waters of his own home.

But when he was healed, his demeanor changed. He who was angry at God suddenly appeared kind; he offered gifts to his prophet and healer. His former anger passed. Kindness moved into his heart, and he was ready to minister to his world.

But the other lepers, unlike Naaman, were not healed. They remained lepers and even though they were diseased, they became agents of healing in the life of Israel. There is a beauty in those who serve God from the center of their afflictions. These are the glorious lepers of grace.

Questions for Personal Reflection

1. In what ways are you a "glorious leper of grace"?

Without God's grace + sacrifice of Jesus I would be nothing. "Without Him I would Be Nothing"—without Him I'd surely fail. W.O Him I would be nothing—like a ship without a sail".

2. Consider your past experiences. How does the healing you have experienced manifest itself in ministry to others?

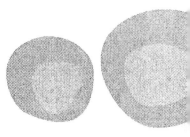

Day 5: My Personal Worship
Read Psalms 137:8–9; 138:1

Prejudice has long, stiff arms that cannot bend. It will not permit us to embrace those we despise for racial or social reasons. Psalm 137 is a poem written by someone whose heart had been stirred by racial abuse at the hands of the Babylonians. Anger, unwashed by grace, burns in the center of this psalm. It sounds odd when such a bitter lament retains its high sense of poetry. Artists can sometimes paint their high indignation, but their art generally suffers. Here in this psalm, the poet wrote beautifully but darkly.

But Psalm 138 erupts in clean, pure praise, remembering that the Babylonians (so hated in Psalm 137) were not God's enemies. Martin Niemöeller, a German and prominent anti-Nazi theologian during World War II, is known to have said that each time Nazi overlords abused him while he was in a concentration camp—shoved him into the mud, slammed his head or body with a rifle butt—he practiced hating them. This continued for a long time until he remembered that while he considered the Nazis to be his enemies, his hatred was not Christlike. This single insight transformed his life and ultimately the whole concentration camp. He learned that kindness was merely anger washed by grace.

Ernest Gordon, a former dean of the chapel at Princeton University, had a similar experience in the valley of the Kwai where he, too, was imprisoned during the Second World War. He had to learn that his torturous Japanese overlords were all God's targets of grace. The entire prison camp was changed when Gordon replaced his resentment with love.

Let us ever guard against prejudice. It is the result of trying to goad God into having our friends as his friends and our enemies as his enemies. There is a better way of seeing people. His way frees us to worship a God who transcends our hang-ups.

Questions for Personal Reflection

1. Are there people toward whom you are likely to feel prejudice? If so, why do you have those feelings? How does God view those you dislike? *as his child*

2. What would help you to see people the way God sees them? *prayer Being around them more to really know them as a friend & see all the good things about them — Sharing w/ them*

Day 6: Aquila & Priscilla—Hospitality Born of Kindness

Read Acts 18:1–4, 18–22, 24–26; Romans 16:3-5; 1 Corinthians 16:19

Priscilla and Aquila appeared six times in the New Testament, and almost every time they were mentioned, they were practicing hospitality. In four of those instances, their home was a center of hospitality. The New Testament era found people traveling empire-wide without many inns or hostels. Priscilla and Aquila supplied a much-needed constant kindness. Consider these Scriptures:

1. *"After this, Paul left Athens and went to Corinth. There he met a Jew named Aquila, a native of Pontus, who had recently come from Italy with his wife Priscilla, because Claudius had ordered all the Jews to leave Rome. Paul went to see them, and because he was a tentmaker as they were, he stayed and worked with them"* (Acts 18:1–3). This the first instance of Aquila and Priscilla showing kindness by opening their home to others.

2. *"Paul stayed on in Corinth for some time. Then he left the brothers and sailed for Syria, accompanied by Priscilla and Aquila"* (v. 18). Here the couple showed themselves hospitable by serving as the apostle's traveling companions.

3. *"Meanwhile a Jew named Apollos, a native of Alexandria, came to Ephesus. He was a learned man, with a thorough knowledge of the Scriptures. He had been instructed in the way of the Lord, and he spoke with great fer-*

vor and taught about Jesus accurately, though he knew only the baptism of John. He began to speak boldly in the synagogue. When Priscilla and Aquila heard him, they invited him to their home and explained to him the way of God more adequately" (vv. 24–26). This gracious couple invited a kind of influential-if-kind heretic into their home for some doctrine lessons.

4. *"Greet Priscilla and Aquila, my fellow workers in Christ Jesus. They risked their lives for me. Not only I but all the churches of the Gentiles are grateful to them. Greet also the church that meets at their house"* (Romans 16:3–5). Here hospitality took the grand leap of self-sacrifice: this couple, who so often opened their home in kindness, now opened their home as a place for a new church to start. Their kindness served in a very hospitable way—church planting.

Blessed be Aquila and Priscilla! The Bible says little about their talents at public speaking or their abilities in evangelism or church administration. We only know they were God's kind hosts, and around their lives all the apostles bowed their heads in reverence.

Questions for Personal Reflection

1. When were you blessed by someone else's hospitality? What did that reveal about that person's relationship with God?

2. What are some ways you can demonstrate hospitality? What should be the goal of your hospitality—to show people what you have or to show people your God?

Day 7: Group Discussion

The following questions should take about forty-five minutes to answer and discuss. Each member should answer the first question, leaving the remaining questions open-ended. Everyone need not answer, but be sure all members participate.

1. *In your experience, what are some damaging effects of anger?*

2. *When have you seen someone's anger affect his or her ability to point other people to God?*

3. *What should you do when you sense your anger intensifying? How does God help when you are angry?* Ask God for help –

4. *Is it possible to be angry and not sin? If so, how would sinless anger be expressed?*

5.   *Why don't some people demonstrate hospitality toward others?*

6.   *What three things can you do to serve other people?*

Week 4: Kindness—Applying the Golden Rule

Memory Passage for the Week: Matthew 7:12

Day 1: Kindness—Applying the Golden Rule

The Golden Rule: Do unto other as you would have them do unto you. Kindness means applying the Golden Rule to all—even those beyond our sociological or ethnic circle. Matthew 15:21–28.

Day 2: The Purpose of God in My Life

The only way to enjoy God's kindness is to repent and allow the Spirit to bring forth the same fruit in one's own life. Judges 1:12–15.

Day 3: My Relationship with Christ

In sending out the apostles on a preaching tour, Jesus reminded them that they were to give the same love and kindness God had given to them. Matthew 10:5–10.

Day 4: My Service to Others

Altars are reared, among other things, as monuments to celebrate the kindness of God. Joshua 22:26–27.

Day 5: My Personal Worship

Jesus counseled us to never go to worship with a grudge in our lives. Matthew 5:21–25.

Day 6: A Character Study on Boaz

Ruth 2:1–23, 3:4–15, 4:9–10

Day 7: Group Discussion

Freely, Freely - song -

Day 1: Kindness—Applying the Golden Rule

Read Matthew 15:21–28 - *Jesus walked to Tyre & Sideon (from Canaan)*

A Gentile woman came in need to Jesus, who was a Jewish field rabbi, to beg a cure for her demoniac daughter. Jesus did not consider the woman "a dog" because she was a "Gentile," but that was the way most Jews of Jesus' day thought of Gentiles.

Prejudice stands in the way of the Golden Rule: do unto others as you would have them do unto you. An old Jewish prayer says, "God, I thank thee that I am not a Gentile, a dog, or a woman." Obviously the prayer was not popular with dogs, Gentiles, or women. Jesus reminded this Syro-Phoenician woman that he was a "Jewish Messiah" sent to the lost sheep of the house of Israel. It wasn't right, said Jesus, to take the doctrinal bread of authentic, theological Judaism and give it to the "dogs."

"Yes," said the woman, "but even dogs are welcome to eat the crumbs that fall from their master's table."

So, Jesus healed her daughter.

Kindness means listening to the hurting even if they are not "our type," or even "our religion." One does not hear Jesus saying to this woman, "It's too bad about your daughter; of course, she is a Canaanite."

Kindness applies the Golden Rule to all, and even those beyond our sociological or ethnic circle. Do unto others as you want them to do unto you; a majestic kindness that changes the world.

Questions for Personal Reflection

1. Who are some of the forgotten people in your community?

2. How can you demonstrate godly kindness to the outcast or forgotten?

Day 2: The Purpose of God in My Life

Read Judges 1:12–15

piece of land
land w - springs of H₂O

Caleb received an inheritance in Canaan. He then passed this inheritance on to his daughter and son-in-law. Similarly, God was rich in kindness, which he manifested throughout the ages by leading sinners to repentance (Romans 2:4).

Later on, what impressed Paul about Jesus was his kindness in removing the yoke of sin and law and replacing it with a yoke that was kind to his shoulders (Matthew 11:29–30). But the only way to enjoy this kindness is to repent and allow the Spirit to bring forth the same fruit in everyday life—otherwise we face the severity of God as the useless branches he trims are "cut off" from his tree (Romans 11:22). At Damascus, Paul responded to the psalmist's invitation; he tasted God's kindness and found it good (Psalm 34:8). As food for the soul, kindness is the pleasantest fruit on the tree of life.

Caleb's life is a study of faithfulness and grace. He survived the Exodus and the desert years during which nearly everyone had died. He received the entire area of Hebron. How could he, who had received so much, ever be stingy? He practiced the Golden Rule hundreds of years before Jesus gave it form and words. And his life became a witness to the ultimate triumph of kindness.

Questions for Personal Reflection

1. When is it easy for you to utilize the Golden Rule? Why is it easy?

2. When is it challenging for you to utilize the Golden Rule? Why is it difficult?

Day 3: My Relationship with Christ

Read Matthew 10:5–10

Jesus sent the disciples out with one overarching principle to guide them: "Freely you have received, freely give" (Matthew 10:8). What was it they had received? Friendship with God's Son; he was the grand offering of their lives. Missionaries essentially have one central message: "We have received the Son, now he is yours."

Is it not the evangelist who drives his church? Freely Jesus came to us, but instead of floodgates of grace, we are dams across the flow. Our cowardice or separation from God short-circuits this system. Cowardice always asks, "What right do I have to impose God's grace on others?" Our separation from God leaves us too remote to remember that God wants to redeem all. He weeps to save those we pass in callous disregard.

This is how we miss Jesus!

Consider the exotic glory that was yours when he came to you. He loved you as you were—a miracle in and of itself. He forgave your sins—a triumph considering that he carried his love for you to the hour of his death. He filled you with his Spirit—a welcome abundance considering that your life was so empty. He gave you a place in his community, filled with souls like yourself who had wandered into wonder; all drank the inebriating love of God. The cost of all this? For you, nothing; for him, everything. Gifts are always free to the receiver, but gifts like his cost the giver everything. Don't be stingy with grace—you got it free, so give it freely.

Questions for Personal Reflection

1. How do you see grace at work in your daily life?

forgiveness

2. When and how can you be an instrument of grace to others?

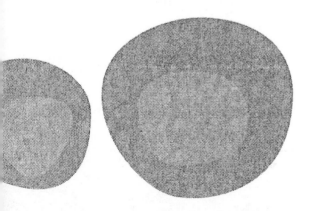

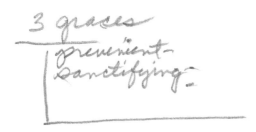

3 graces
prevenient-
sanctifying-

Day 4: My Service to Others

Read Joshua 22:26–27

The tribes east of the Jordan had raised an altar so they would never forget the faith they shared with their brother tribes west of the Jordan. When the other Israelites understood these intentions, they blessed their brother tribes as they celebrated a common legacy.

In Joshua 4:21–22, Joshua built a similar altar and told Israel that in future years when their children asked, "What do these stones mean?" they were to answer with their testament of grace.

Altars are reared as monuments—among other things—to celebrate the kindness of God. I never see the Lincoln Memorial without remembering this presidential martyr. It is said that an African-American mother and her daughter passed the funeral bier where the dead president lay in state. The mother said to her daughter, "Take a good, long, look at that man, sweetie. He died for you."

The Lincoln Memorial always reminds me of that story. It is a story of kindness, and that memorial is a monument of grace. Altars should celebrate kindness and should motivate us to follow in others' virtuous footsteps.

Questions for Personal Reflection

1. What are you doing to leave God's mark on your family, community, and world? *I hope enough to leave a small mark.*

2. What events remind you of God's grace and love for you? How can you relate those stories to those who have never heard?

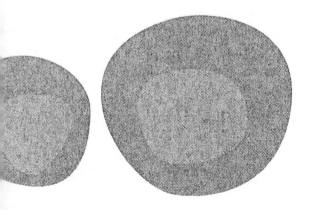

Day 5: My Personal Worship
Read Matthew 5:21–25

Worship is a place of trans-realm relationships. Worship is where we bring our cleansed hearts to put them in concord with God's immaculate holiness. And so we approach him, having set our thirst for holiness and right relationships out front for all to consider. But what if some find a blemish on our deportment, a smudge of some intentional fault? What then?

Jesus said we must not enter into the adoration of a holy God carrying grudges of hate. So we must leave our gift unoffered and go find those with whom we have any grievance, and straighten out our world of relationships. When we have done our best to mend our broken world, we may return to the altar and offer praise. God loves the whole world, and when we allow ourselves to have a grudge toward any of his children, we cannot meet with him in open communion. God wants his family to have no subterfuge going on. Peace in the family is what every loving father wants.

A certain man of my acquaintance was about to have all his children home for a Christmas reunion. Before they came, he told them up front that he wanted only one gift that Christmas: for his children to love each other throughout the whole Christmas season.

Similarly, every public worship service is a meeting of the family of God. It is God's desire as head of the family that we give him one present above all—a universal love for the entire family he loves. There is no use giving God such sundry gifts as our tithes when we have not given him the first gift of loving all his other children.

Questions for Personal Reflection

1. What relationships need to be mended before you worship God?

2. How can God use you to bring healing and unity in the midst of strife and trouble?

Day 6: Boaz—Kindness as a Sign of Romance

Read Ruth 2:1-23; 3:4–15; 4:9–10

In this desperate tale of romance, Naomi returned to Bethlehem with her daughter-in-law. Steeped in poverty, Ruth gleaned the fields of a wealthy young Bethlehemite farmer named Boaz. It appeared to be love at first sight, for upon merely seeing her, Boaz asked, "Whose young woman is that?" (Ruth 2:5). When he found that she was a gleaner and a foreigner, his interest in her only seemed to increase, and he approached her and showed her—over the next few weeks—nine specific kindnesses:

First, he said to her, "Don't go and glean in another field" (v. 8),

Second, he ordered the field hands not to take any sexual liberties with Ruth, since she was a foreign woman living in a strange land with no protector (v. 9).

Third, he told her that whenever she got thirsty she could drink from the refreshing jars that he kept for his own field hands (v. 9).

Fourth, he complimented her on the excellent kindness she showed her mother-in-law, Naomi (v. 11).

Fifth, he allowed her to share the noon meal with the people he had hired (v. 14).

Sixth, (and now we know this is getting serious) he ordered the harvesters to drop grain on purpose so she wouldn't have to work so hard to find it (v. 16).

Seventh, he protected her reputation after she spent the night with him on the threshing floor (her mother-in-law's suggestion, by the way); he was concerned that her dignity not be smudged by insinuation (Ruth 3:14).

Eighth, he gave her six measures of barley just as a present—a very valuable present in their time of hardship (v. 15).

Finally, he bought her hand in marriage by outbidding the kinsman-redeemer who was in first place (Ruth 4:1–10).

So this love affair, which began with kindness, was consummated in romance. The child born to them was an ancestor of our Lord. Hear what might have been Boaz's sonnet:

There in the gold she stands, empress of grain,
The harvest just ahead of her. I see
And in this glance I know why lovers die
For love. I own these fields, this realm she reigns.
She stops. Those almond eyes of Araby
Survey her new-found home. Oh God she's come
This alien immigrant of majesty
And Isaac stares at Ishmael as dumb.
Bethlehem is charged. The desert's green.
Such fields as these might angels know in time
Such beauty might conceive a royal king
Such regal bearing tempts the light to shine.
May Moab mother infant princes here
And love be mine while ages stand and cheer.

Questions for Personal Reflection

1. Some say God's love for us is a classic example of romance because he pursues us relentlessly. How has God pursued you?

2. What are some things you do to pursue others for God?

pray, invite to church, speak to them about God & what He has done for me -

Day 7: Group Discussion

The following questions should take about forty-five minutes to answer and discuss. Each member should answer the first question, leaving the remaining questions open-ended. Everyone need not answer, but be sure all members participate.

1. *Who in your life is hurting and what are you doing to listen to them?*

2. *Authentic listening leads to action. As you listen to the hurting, how should you respond?* Pray w/ them right then Help to work out a plan of action in which you can be a help to the one hurting. Get involved.

3. *What can you do to make the Golden Rule more of a reality in your life?*

4. *How would you summarize God's purpose for your life? How are you living out that purpose?*

To bring honor & glory to His name through my actions and love for others.

5. *Hate undermines our ability to worship God. How have you seen hate affect true worship?* L V

6. *How does Ruth portray God's love for us? What should be our response to God's love?* When all the men in Naomi's family died Ruth "would not leave her" - I will not leave you nor forsake you. She would give her life for her. She should love and kindness to her mother-in-law in her time of need
"barley + wheat harvest"

— Francine Rigers

Week 5: Kindness—The Approach to Grace

Memory Passage for the Week: Psalm 18:49–50

Day 1: Kindness—The Approach to Grace

Martin Luther wrote that Jesus' kindness is but God's approach to grace; we would do well to emulate that kindness. 1 Samuel 25:32–35.

Day 2: The Purpose of God in My Life

Exodus tells the story of how Hebrew midwives were kind—even when they knew their kindness might cost them their lives. Exodus 1:19–21.

Day 3: My Relationship with Christ

We must take notice of not only the smaller, everyday kindnesses of God but the really great kindness that he, in Christ, reconciled. Job 10:8–12.

Day 4: My Service to Others

Kindness is the key that opens the world to the message of Christ. Proverbs 11:16–17.

Day 5: My Personal Worship

In the overwhelming presence of God's grace and kindness, we must fall down in worship. Ephesians 2:6–10.

Day 6: The Parable of the Good Samaritan

Luke 10:25–37 (TLB)

Day 7: Group Discussion

Day 1: Kindness—The Approach to Grace

Read 1 Samuel 25:32–35

David blessed Abigail for helping him be moderate when he was in a mood for vengeance. Kindness is a virtue that sometimes arrives too late, after we have enjoyed being as mad as we wanted to be for as long as we wanted to be.

Abigail reminded David that unnecessarily killing his enemies was not a measure of God's kindness. Martin Luther wrote that Jesus' kindness is but God's approach to grace, and we would do well to emulate Jesus' kindness.

> *Christ gives you faith with all its benefits, and you are to give your neighbor love with all its benefits. You may ask then what are the good works that you should do for your neighbor? They have no name just as the good works that Christ did for you have no name ... they have no name for this reason: lest they be divided and this be done and that be left undone. Rather you must give yourself to your neighbor utterly, just as Christ did confine himself to prayer and fasting for you.... So this is not your good work, that you should give alms or pray, but rather that you should give yourself entirely to your neighbor, as he needs and you can, with alms, prayers, fasting, counsel, comfort, teaching, ap-*

peal, reproof, pardon, clothes, food, and also suffering and death on his behalf. But tell me where in all Christendom are such works?[3]

Luther was asking where kindness exists in our world. It is noticeably infrequent. Where are the Abigails who stay our hands and tempers and beg us to be kind to our enemies? Wouldn't such kindness make a place for God's grace in a world that looks to be loved and finds very few lovers?

Questions for Personal Reflection

1. How is God's kindness revealed to you? How do you respond?

2. What are some ways in which you might "kill" your enemies? How does "killing your enemies" affect their openness to the message of Jesus Christ?

Day 2: The Purpose of God in My Life

Read Exodus 1:19–21

The Hebrew midwives were ordinary women who probably never considered themselves heroes—yet they did a most heroic thing. When commanded to be cruel, they acted kindly. They knew God was the God of protecting life, not destroying it. The kindness of these women in their brutal world was as refreshing as it was surprising. Such kindness has said its prayers and has courage. Kindness that practices grace in a world where grace is forbidden is definitely God's sort of kindness.

Exiled Soviet novelist Solzhenitsyn said that his faith in Christ came to be because of one of his doctors, Doctor Kornpett, who was a Christian. The doctor's consistent kindness first impressed Solzhenitsyn, and later caused him to believe in Christ.

During the Cuban revolution, one of my very good friends was incarcerated for four years, during which he ministered to his fellow inmates in extraordinary ways. One of those ways was by taking his Spanish New Testament—the only one in the prison—tearing it into six equal parts and then operating a surreptitious lending library of New Testament fragments out of his jail cell. Of course, this kindness was against the rules, but the ministry it brought to his fellow believers was a kindness that endured in their memories for the rest of their lives.

To this day, I am baffled by my friend's courage. I think it's because he doesn't seem particularly heroic to me. I feel sure he doesn't seem heroic to himself. But his kindness is unmistakable. He has taught me that where courage and kindness make friends, the grace of God is apt to transform the world—whether on the birthing stools of Egypt, in a Cuban prison, or for that matter, in the center of any of our lives.

Questions for Personal Reflection

1. In what ways have you seen courage come forth in kindness?

2. How can you be more courageous and, as a result, more kind?

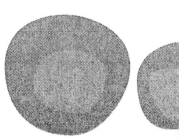

Day 3: My Relationship with Christ
Read Job 10:8–12

The ability to breathe is an act of God's kindness. The formation of a fetus is an act of God's kindness. Skin is an act of God's kindness. Job stopped and celebrated these ordinary things, teaching us how very extraordinary they are.

Grace saves us, but is it not also grace that creates us, feeds us, sees that our children arrive safely in the world, and gives us a hot slice of bread on a cold January day?

Grace, grace, grace—kindness, kindness, kindness: distinguish these for me if you can. But when you have tried, I will still, like Job, often find them indistinguishable.

Here is my litany of grace, and as I speak it I turn to celebrate with every phrase my relationship with Christ:

> *Dear Christ,*
> *With every slice of warm bread, I praise your name.*
> *For rain on a warm evening and the smell of ground, I praise your name.*
> *For a child's laughter and a woman's lullaby, I praise your name.*
> *For the Word of God, the word of novelists, for my own words,*
> *For the stars when I can see them and when I can't,*
> *For the truth when if can figure it out and when I can't,*
> *For a robed choir and one who can't afford robes,*

For preachers who use pulpits and those who don't,

For barefoot on warm concrete and barefoot in the park,

For barefoot on carpet and barefoot in mountain brooks,

For barefoot before the fire and barefoot on in the rain:

For all things, I measure your kindness and I thank you.

Questions for Personal Reflection

1. What are your thoughts when you consider God's kindness and grace?

2. Spend a few moments meditating on God's grace allowing it to overwhelm

your cares and concerns. What parts of your life need a fresh touch from God?

Day 4: My Service to Others
Read Proverbs 11:16–17

This passage deals with a kindhearted woman in love with a hard-hearted man. There is an old country-western song that pursues the same theme. And oddly enough they end up at the same place. We are forced to admire the kindhearted woman, but not the hard-hearted man. This passage uses the word *ruthless*—a word that not only isn't kind but is actually cruel.

Kindness is quite the opposite of ruthlessness, as it makes a way for grace and the service of others. It is said that Evangeline Booth, the fourth general of the Salvation Army, rescued a homeless woman from the sidewalks. In her day such homeless souls were called "guttersnipes," but she took the woman into one of the Salvation Army hostels and began to care for her. The woman was comatose and did not revive for several hours. But she did regain consciousness just as Evangeline Booth leaned over and kissed her ... and apparently kissed her awake. To which the woman responded, "Thank you for doing that. Ain't nobody done that since my mama died."

Kind people care when those around them hurt. Ruthless people do not. I suppose it goes without saying that ruthless people don't become this way intentionally—it is not a life goal. Ruthlessness happens gradually to people who forget to practice random acts of kindness.

Grace that saves sometimes waits for kindness to pave the way. If you want to win people to Christ, steep yourself in kindness.

Questions for Personal Reflection

1. Maybe your first encounter with Christ was wrapped in someone else's kindness. If so, describe that time. If not, describe how you came to first experience the authentic love of God.

2. How can you offer kindness to the downcast in your community?

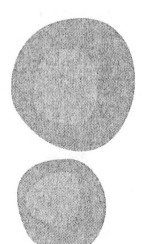

Day 5: My Personal Worship

Read Ephesians 2:6–10

This passage in Ephesians must be the epitome of correlating kindness, grace, and saving faith. These three are bound together inseparably in this passage. It is too lovely to be prosaic about, so let me set it in verse:

> *God raised up Christ and seated him above*
> *In places so majestic we but wonder*
> *"Is there any edge to heaven's love?*
> *Is there any realm of grace above or under*
> *Where he might now or in some part of space*
> *Reveal to us the reason for such grace?"*

> *Kindness came and dressed in rich humility,*
> *It drew eternity toward my time,*
> *And I stare bewildered that it all is free,*
> *And Christ, the cosmic Lord, is friends with me.*

> *Saved by faith, by grace and naught of me.*
> *Yet purchased as a present from love's sea—*
> *So wide and deep and free I marvel yet*
> *At love that bled and saved without regret.*

Questions for Personal Reflection

1. As you read the poem, what thoughts came to mind?

2. How can the truths of this poem become reality in your daily life?

Day 6: The Parable of the Good Samaritan

LUKE 10:25-37 (TLB)

One day an expert on Moses' laws came to test Jesus' orthodoxy by asking him this question: "Teacher, what does a man need to do to live forever in heaven?"

Jesus replied, "What does Moses' law say about it?"

"It says," he replied, "that you must love the Lord your God with all your heart, and with all your soul, and with all your strength, and with all your mind. And you must love your neighbor just as much as you love yourself."

"Right!" Jesus told him. "Do this and you shall live!"

The man wanted to justify (his lack of love for some kinds of people), so he asked, "Which neighbors?"

Jesus replied with an illustration: "A Jew going on a trip from Jerusalem to Jericho was attacked by bandits. They stripped him of his clothes and money and beat him up and left him lying half dead beside the road.

"By chance a Jewish priest came along: and when he saw the man lying there, he crossed to the other side of the road and passed him by. A Jewish temple-assistant walked over and looked at him there, but then went on.

"But a despised Samaritan came along, and when he saw him, he felt deep pity. Kneeling beside him, the Samaritan soothed his wounds with medicine and bandaged them. Then he put the man on his donkey and walked along beside him till they came to an inn, where he nursed him through the night. The next day he handed the innkeeper two twenty-dollar bills and told him to take care of the man. 'If his bill runs any higher than that,' he said, 'I'll pay the difference the next time I am here.'

"Now which of these three would you say was a neighbor to the bandits' victim?"

The man replied, "The one who showed him some pity."

Then Jesus said, "Yes, now go and do the same."

Questions for Personal Reflection

1. Reread the parable and determine which person best represents the way in which you respond to people in need.

2. What does it mean to be a neighbor? How does your life compare to the biblical example of neighborliness?

Day 7: Group Discussion

The following questions should take about forty-five minutes to answer and discuss. Each member should answer the first question, leaving the remaining questions open-ended. Everyone need not answer, but be sure all members participate.

1. *What is grace and how have you experienced it?*

2. *How has God's kindness helped you better understand his grace?*

3. *Consider some of the ways in which you have seen God's grace in action. How might God's grace work through you to lead others to him?*

4. *What are some ways your small group can work together to meet the needs of others in your church and community?*

5. *How does the world respond when we attribute something to God's grace?*

6. *How can God's grace enable us to grow stronger in our faith and more committed in our service to him?*

Week 6: The Good Samaritan—Kindness Personified

Memory Passage for the Week: 1 Thessalonians 5:15

Day 1: The Good Samaritan—Kindness Personified

The story of the Good Samaritan transcends heavy theological definitions of kindness for a richer, more fulfilling illustration. Luke 10:25–37.

Day 2: The Purpose of God in My Life

Just quoting Scripture is not enough: we must live out God's Word. And how can we live it? One primary way is through showing kindness. Luke 10:25–28.

Day 3: My Relationship with Christ

The Samaritan, whose name is not known to us, showed how a relationship with Christ should produce within us the kindness to love our neighbors as ourselves. Luke 10:29.

Day 4: My Service to Others

Kindness is the work of neighborliness, and neighborliness is the heartbeat of our service to others. Luke 10:36.

Day 5: My Personal Worship

When we touch others with kindness, we have issued a great *Alleluia!* Even better than any we might read from a hymnal or prayer book. Luke 10:37.

Day 6: Verses for Further Reflection

Day 7: Group Discussion

Day 1: The Good Samaritan—Kindness Personified

Read Luke 10:25–37

The proud are rarely kind. Perhaps this is because egotistical thinking uses up too much of their time. It was the despised Samaritan in Jesus' parable who, having no reason to be proud, could think of no reason why he should not serve. Only the "unproud" can become humility at work— kindness personified. Every once in a while we meet such wonderful, rather Samaritan, believers. Often they are persons of some age and wisdom, who act out the virtue of kindness and call the quarreling world around them to peace. They have lived through trials, but the brutality of their years has settled as an aura of gold around them. To have them walk into the room says to all present: "Hold your tempers, quit all criticism: the Savior's lovers are in our midst, and we must, for conscience's sake, learn what they know. We will be kind. To be anything other than kind in their presence is to deny the work of God."

Jesus' best example of kindness was the Good Samaritan. I doubt the Good Samaritan credited himself for his fine example, because I believe kindness was a fixed part of his lifestyle. He probably never noticed how noble he was as he went about doing good for others. In this regard he was probably different from many "church people". Instead of a demonstration of kindness, church people often hand out some verse of Scripture or a long exposition on what some theologian had to say about kindness. But in this lesson on kindness, Jesus was asked a serious question regarding how people inherit eternal life. His answer was at first what you might expect from a theologian—really from one theologian to another.

The other theologian in this tale was a "lawyer and theologian," one who was especially adept at interpreting the Torah. This thinker gave Jesus an answer from the Torah. There was nothing wrong with the lawyer's answer, and Jesus in no way criticized him. However, while the lawyer's answer was biblical and honest, it was not all that fulfilling. So Jesus set out on a story that became one of the great stories of the Western world.

The truth of Jesus' story is so abundant that in reading it, heavy theological definitions of kindness are forced to abandon their plodding ways and take flight. Buoyant with kindness, they fly with a joyous humanity.

Questions for Personal Reflection

1. When was a time when you were right but not very nice?

2. When was a time when honest questions were being asked with no motive at all for being kind?

Day 2: The Purpose of God in My Life

Read Luke 10:25–28

It's a mighty question: "What must I do to inherit eternal life?" (Luke 10:25). Jesus responded with a question: "What is written in the law?" (v. 26). The lawyer, an "expert" in the law, answered Jesus' question by quoting the Old Testament:

> *Love the LORD your God with all your heart*
> *and with all your soul*
> *and with all your strength.*
> —Deuteronomy 6:5

And he added,

> *Love your neighbor as yourself.*
> —Leviticus 19:18

Jesus complimented this expert in the law on his good theology. But what does this passage really mean? The statement really implies that kindness is a primary purpose of God in our lives. But just quoting Scripture is not enough: we have to live it. And how can we live it? One primary way is through showing kindness.

Kindness is more than a good deed here or there. Kindness is a reflection of God's love in our hearts. We all fail to be kind at times. We all sin. We need God's love in our hearts in order to love others properly—the way the Good Samaritan did. If we can see that while there may not be much good or kindness in us, if we put our faith in the Good Shepherd, his godly kindness inhabits us and becomes our own. We, too, can be Good Samaritans.

When the Holy Spirit dwells in us

Questions for Personal Reflection

1. Have you known someone who seemed to have all the right answers, but all the wrong practices? What was the nature of this conflict?

2. Does God's presence help you to be more kind to those around you? *yes* If not, how could you improve?

Day 3: My Relationship with Christ
Read Luke 10:29

"Who is my neighbor?" the lawyer asked Jesus (Luke 10:29). It must have struck Jesus as odd that a man who knew the Ten Commandments and all the laws, as this man did, had trouble knowing who his neighbor was. Jesus didn't give the lawyer a dictionary definition of *neighbor*. Instead, he told the lawyer the story of a kind man—the Good Samaritan. While dictionary definitions may be forgettable, stories seldom are.

With the story of the Good Samaritan, Jesus demonstrated that a neighbor is not just someone who lives nearby; a neighbor is anyone in need. Here Jesus widened the concept of "neighbor" to say that you can't claim to love your neighbor if you only love those who live near you. We must go out of our way to love our neighbors, for that may be exactly where they are—out of our way. It is their need, not their geography, that commands our service. The Good Samaritan helped a hurting man he didn't even know. Not his next-door neighbor, but a complete stranger. How Christlike!

All God's children are our neighbors. And the Samaritan, whose name is not known, showed how a relationship with Christ should produce the kindness to love our neighbors as ourselves. We must pray that our relationship with Christ grows wide enough to engulf the wounded in our way.

Questions for Personal Reflection

1. Describe a time when God commanded you to lay down your prejudice and act in compassion?

2. In the next week, how might you be kind to someone you previously overlooked?

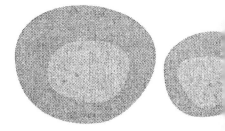

Day 4: My Service to Others
Read Luke 10:36

Induction is a style of teaching that requires the student to answer the question, rather than letting the teacher answer it for him or her. Jesus was a master of induction, using the Good Samaritan's tale as a teaching tool. He never really answered the lawyer's question; he asked the question again after he finished the story and forced the lawyer to answer it himself. Questions others answer for us are never as fixed in our soul as those with which we must grapple ourselves.

There was nothing wrong with the lawyer's answer, and Jesus in no way criticized him. However, the question the lawyer should have answered was: *How can I use this occasion to magnify my calling as it relates to my service to others?* But after Jesus finished his story, the whole issue of kindness had doubled back upon itself. And the story ended right where it began: "Which of these three do you think was a neighbor?" (Luke 10:36).

Ministry to others is a nearer path to heaven than just keeping the commandments and being an expert in theology. The lawyer had his question ripped from the pages of his theology books and placed rather powerfully in a basin and towel. And the answer to his question must have stuck with him: kindness is the work of neighborliness. As simple as it sounds, neighborliness is the heartbeat of our service to others.

Questions for Personal Reflection

1. What is more important to you—your theology or the way you treat others?

2. Can you think of a time when your actions were biblical but not very kind?

NO

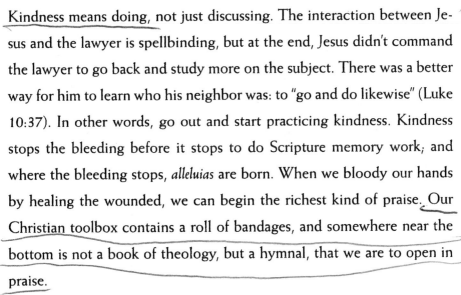

Day 5: My Personal Worship
Read Luke 10:37

Kindness means doing, not just discussing. The interaction between Jesus and the lawyer is spellbinding, but at the end, Jesus didn't command the lawyer to go back and study more on the subject. There was a better way for him to learn who his neighbor was: to "go and do likewise" (Luke 10:37). In other words, go out and start practicing kindness. Kindness stops the bleeding before it stops to do Scripture memory work; and where the bleeding stops, *alleluias* are born. When we bloody our hands by healing the wounded, we can begin the richest kind of praise. Our Christian toolbox contains a roll of bandages, and somewhere near the bottom is not a book of theology, but a hymnal, that we are to open in praise.

In Philippians Paul celebrates the kindness of the Philippian church. His letter says, in effect, that kindness begets kindness. And when kindness is in place, Christians really do help each other through dark and discouraging times. The apostle, who received kindness from the Philippians, responded with kindness. And the little epistle explodes with the apostle's praise.

One cold December I was ministering outdoors to my congregation in a very light and inadequate jacket. Afterward, a church member anonymously sent me a beautifully lined and warm leather coat. I was struck by an overwhelming desire to repay this kindness. However, I had not the slightest idea of who my benefactor was. It is an uncomfortable feeling to be the "blessee" and not know who the "blesser" was. As a result, I found myself being nice—very nice—to just about everyone. The only way I could reply to so kind a gift was to show kindness to the whole congregation. The gift overwhelmed my need—what could I do but praise the Lord? You see, kindness also begets worship.

Questions for Personal Reflection

1. How does Jesus and the lawyer's conversation correlate with James 1:22, which says: "Do not merely listen to the word, and so deceive yourselves. Do what it says"?

2. Have you ever praised God as a result of someone's kindness to you? Describe that occasion.

Day 6: Verses for Further Reflection

Matthew 7:12: In everything, do to others what you would have them do to you, for this sums up the Law and the Prophets.

Luke 6:35: But love your enemies, do good to them, and lend to them without expecting to get anything back. Then your reward will be great, and you will be sons of the Most High, because he is kind to the ungrateful and wicked.

Romans 2:4: Or do you show contempt for the riches of his kindness, tolerance and patience, not realizing that God's kindness leads you toward repentance?

Romans 11:22: Consider therefore the kindness and sternness of God: sternness to those who fell, but kindness to you, provided that you continue in his kindness. Otherwise, you also will be cut off.

2 Corinthians 6:4, 6: Rather, as servants of God we commend ourselves in every way: in great endurance; in troubles, hardships and distresses; ... in purity, understanding, patience and kindness; in the Holy Spirit and in sincere love.

Ephesians 2:6-7: And God raised us up with Christ and seated us with him in the heavenly realms in Christ Jesus, in order that in the coming ages he might show the incomparable riches of his grace, expressed in his kindness to us in Christ Jesus.

PHILIPPIANS 1:3–9; 2:19–30

In this passage Paul celebrated the kindness of the Philippian church and the truth that kindness begets kindness. Somehow when kindness is in place Christians help each other through dark and discouraging times.

I thank my God every time I remember you. In all my prayers for all of you, I always pray with joy because of your partnership in the gospel from the first day until now, being confident of this, that he who began a good work in you will carry it on to completion until the day of Christ Jesus.

It is right for me to feel this way about all of you, since I have you in my heart; for whether I am in chains or defending and confirming the gospel, all of you share in God's grace with me. God can testify how I long for all of you with the affection of Christ Jesus.

And this is my prayer: that your love may abound more and more in knowledge and depth of insight....

I hope in the Lord Jesus to send Timothy to you soon, that I also may be cheered when I receive news about you. I have no one else like him, who takes a genuine interest in your welfare. For everyone looks out for his own interests, not those of Jesus Christ. But you know that Timothy has proved himself, because as a son with his father he has served with me in the work of the gospel.

I hope, therefore, to send him as soon as I see how things go with me. And I am confident in the Lord that I myself will come soon.

But I think it is necessary to send back to you Epaphroditus, my brother, fellow worker and fellow soldier, who is also your messenger, whom you sent to take care of my needs. For he longs for all of you and is distressed because you heard he was ill. Indeed he was ill, and almost died. But God had mercy on him, and not on him only but also on me, to spare me sorrow upon sorrow. Therefore I am all the more eager to send him, so that when you see him again you may be glad and I may have less anxiety. Welcome him in the Lord with great joy, and honor men like him, because he almost died for the work of Christ, risking his life to make up for the help you could not give me.

Questions for Personal Reflection

1. Paul's ministry was possible because believers invested their resources in him. In what kinds of things are you investing your resources? *The missions of our church - toothbrushes, toothpaste*

2. Sometimes we can't physically go on a mission, but we can enable others to go. What can you do to further the reach of the gospel from where you are? *monitary gifts - fundraisers, prayers -*

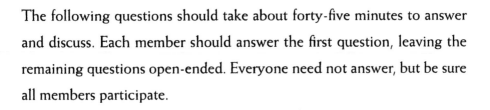

Day 7: Group Discussion

The following questions should take about forty-five minutes to answer and discuss. Each member should answer the first question, leaving the remaining questions open-ended. Everyone need not answer, but be sure all members participate.

1. *How does the spread of the gospel in the early church compare to the way in which we spread the gospel now?*

2. *What were some positive traits that resulted from Paul's experiences?*
    kindness, generousity, hospitality.

3. *How does ministry to others affect your overall spiritual health?*

    more relaxed when you know you have helped your neighbor –

4. *How is your life encouraging others in their service to God?*

5. *How are others drawn closer to God or driven away from him by the actions of Christians?* When others *experience* see kindness in Christians Christians that ~~they feel have~~ quote scripture, talk about coming to church — — — —

6. *How are you working to develop kindness in your life?*

Just trying to ~~realize~~ recognize situations in which I can use kindness to help someone through hard times.

ENDNOTES

1. *Calvin Miller,* A Symphony in Sand *(Waco, TX: Word, 1990) 100–101.*

2. *Calvin Miller,* An Owner's Manual for the Unfinished Soul *(Wheaton, IL: Harold Shaw Publishers, 1997) 86.*

PRAYER JOURNAL

Use the following pages to record both prayer requests and answers.

Kelly McDowell - granddaughter (16) of Shirley
Lindholm & disfunctional household - panic attacks
Sissy - no glowing, but mass is larger -
Dr. wants her to take more chemo, but -
Goes to lung Dr. next wk.   no -
Pray for church & for workers for
Math Madness -
Delete Lloyd -
Ruth Garrard

PRAYER JOURNAL